Broken and Beautiful

Broken and Beautiful

31 Days from Healing to Joy

Julie Woodley
Foreword by Robert V. Rakestraw

RESOURCE *Publications* • Eugene, Oregon

BROKEN AND BEAUTIFUL
31 Days from Healing to Joy

Copyright © 2016 Julie Woodley. All rights reserved. Except for brief quotations in critical publications or reviews, no part of this book may be reproduced in any manner without prior written permission from the publisher. Write: Permissions, Wipf and Stock Publishers, 199 W. 8th Ave., Suite 3, Eugene, OR 97401.

Resource Publications
An Imprint of Wipf and Stock Publishers
199 W. 8th Ave., Suite 3
Eugene, OR 97401

www.wipfandstock.com

PAPERBACK ISBN: 978-1-5326-0229-0
HARDCOVER ISBN: 978-1-5326-0231-3
EBOOK ISBN: 978-1-5326-0230-6

Manufactured in the U.S.A.   SEPTEMBER 28, 2016

Scripture quotations are taken from the *Holy Bible*, New International Version®, NIV®, unless otherwise noted. Copyright © 1973, 1978, 1984, 2011 by Biblica, Inc.™ Used by permission of Zondervan. All rights reserved worldwide. www.zondervan.com The "NIV" and "New International Version" are trademarks registered in the United States Patent and Trademark Office by Biblica, Inc.™

Scripture quotations marked (NLT) are taken from the *Holy Bible*, New Living Translation, copyright ©1996, 2004, 2007, 2013 by Tyndale House Foundation. Used by permission of Tyndale House Publishers, Inc., Carol Stream, Illinois 60188. All rights reserved.

Scripture taken from the New King James Version®. Copyright © 1982 by Thomas Nelson. Used by permission. All rights reserved.

Scripture quotations marked (KJV) are taken from the Holy Bible, King James Version (Public Domain).

I dedicate this devotional to the many Wildflowers that our ministry has been able to faithfully reach. You are my heroes! From Africa, to Ireland, to the rural communities and big cities in the United States, there are Wildflowers blooming everywhere. I love you all. Dare to hope again. God has an incredible plan for you and me; let's reach out and plant other Wildflowers.

Contents

Forward by Robert V. Rakestraw, PhD | ix

Acknowledgments | xi

Introduction | xiii

Hearing God | 1

Broken and Powerful | 2

Come to the Party! | 3

Prepared for Battle | 4

Determined to Listen | 5

Dwelling in Weakness | 6

Finding Courage in Love | 7

The Powerful Wounded | 8

Love Revolutionaries | 9

Victory Banner | 10

By His Grace | 11

From Devastation to Joy | 12

From Disaster to Desire | 13

Provision in Disruption | 14

Fight and Don't Grow Weary | 15

Where I Meet the Lord | 16

Filling Up the Canyon | 17

Greater Possibilities of Love | 18

Beyond Making Life Work | 19

Go and Be Blessed | 20

Third Heaven | 21

Joy Remains | 22

Worship in My Tears | 23

Free Indeed | 24

Defined by the Mess No More | 25

Unlikely and Amazing | 26

Victory from Faith | 27

Face the Anxiety | 28

Depravity Defeated | 29

Living in the Seam | 30

Breathtaking on the Edge | 31

Foreword

THESE HIGHLY PERSONAL DEVOTIONAL writings of Julie Woodley come from a quietly bubbling, potent, and beautiful fountain – one fed by three streams deep within her heart and mind.

One stream consists of her terribly painful memories of childhood abuse: verbal, physical, sexual, and emotional. These ugly memories no longer torment Julie, but they cannot be easily erased.

A second stream flows from her intimate life in God. Because she has come to know, by long experience, the remarkable love and healing power of her Lord and Savior, she enjoys a closeness with God that overpowers her and fills her daily with childlike trust and joy.

A third stream that continually feeds the life-giving fountain that is Julie Woodley is an unquenchable compassion for hurting people. Because Julie has come from a place of extremely deep hurt that once led her to the very brink of suicide, she engages in a relentless, Christ-focused pursuit of healing and restoration for those shattered and nearly destroyed by the crushing blows of life. She is for sure a wounded healer of many — one who relies totally on her heavenly Father for daily grace and direction.

I definitely recommend these readings — intended to be read meditatively — from this strong and transparent woman of God whom I have been privileged to know and support in ministry for over a quarter century.

Robert V. Rakestraw, PhD
Professor of Theology Emeritus
Bethel Seminary, St. Paul, MN
Author and Editor
Founder and Director, Grace Quest Ministries

Acknowledgments

THANK YOU TO so many incredible women who have breathed truth and love into my heart:

Thank you Sharon Goding. You are closer than a sister; you are part of my heart!

Faith Frederick—you are so loving and faithful—you have taught me how to be a feminine warrior.

Dr. Jeanette Bakke, your words and prayers have nurtured me so. From the day I entered seminary with you as my professor, I knew my life would never be the same.

Jeanette Vought, you mentored, loved, and gave me support in the hardest times.

Mary Lowman—a new friend, but I have a beautiful prediction of years of support and prayers to come.

I could list hundreds of beautiful wildflowers that have impacted my life—thank you each and every one.

But one beautiful woman who left this world 30 years ago made the deepest love impact and legacy. With tears of love, I thank you my Grandmother Eileen.

You taught me how to love like no other. You displayed extravagant love and mentored and parented me each step of the way. Much of the time you were quiet in the way you shaped me, but I watched you Grandma! I watched you give; I watched you forgive; I watched you love—sometimes when the person didn't deserve it. As you used to say about yourself, "I may not be very pretty; I may not be very smart; but I can love better than anyone" and that you could, my dearest Grandmother! If I can be a small

Acknowledgments

reflection of the kindness and grace you gave others, then I will be ecstatic with joy.

I'm excited to see you in heaven and tell you of all the people that I have loved with the love you gave to me, because we both know all this love was from God. You were filled with Him. I'll continue the love revolution here on earth until I come to heaven with you. I promise you one of those big squishy hugs and wet kisses you gave me so generously!

Introduction

As I wrote this devotional, I prayed that it would be a prayer meeting between the Lord, myself, and you. God provided a buffer zone, so I could enter into silence and focus on things unseen. Then, I could bring his Glory to the tangible world and share those revelations with eyes that see and ears that hear.

The chaos and violence in this world, and in the lives of those who seek help, affords us the great opportunity to speak God's truth into these matters. I have asked Jesus for the courage to speak truth, the wisdom of God to do it well, and the grace to remember that as God speaks to me, it's not just for others, but for my sake too. As Oswald Chambers said in My Utmost for His Highest, I pray I may "be careful to maintain strenuously God's point of view" (from his devotion for October 24, based on 2 Corinthians 2:14)

Jesus, My heart is yours! I give you my trust and I give you my life! My heart is moved, stirred, and romanced. The vessel called my heart is bursting with love, life, hope and pure joy. Your love, Oh Lord, sings within me—in my dreams, in my visions, in the twilight, in my waking, in the darkness and in the light — all day and all night. I pray the undercurrent of who I am is you. I am filled with wild love — overwhelming, saturating, and transforming. I desire that you may be caught up in this wild love too.

All I have to offer is my weakness and I know He brings his loving strength into my weakness! I have been in many turbulent storms. In the chaos and the pain, God has been so faithful. He may not have answered all my questions, but he has been with me in each

Introduction

and every moment, every step of the way. He has been (and still is) an incredible travel companion, my abiding presence always.

Thank you for entering into this 31-day journey with me. Oh, the places we will travel and the people we shall meet. All we have to offer the wounded is a Savior that understands their scars and longs to reach into their lives with healing love. I have experienced the reality of that healing love to the depths of who I am. You are not alone, dear one; He goes before you. Enter into this 31-day adventure wide open to His kindness and grace.

Love,
God's Wildflower
Julie

Hearing God

Speak, Lord, for your servant is listening. (1 Samuel 3:9)

This place that God has me in—this vulnerable, dependent space where I find pure beauty and joy—has awakened my heart to do something more.

It reminds me that the world is dying to know and experience this kind of extravagant love as well. The more I give away, the more He gives in abundance. The love revolution continues. I am no longer locking my heart away in the attic of daily obligations. I'm no longer silencing my deepest longings.

I am overwhelmed with the generosity that my Lord showers on me every day. It's an over-abundance of real love! He has created me to share this heroic intimacy.

Broken and Powerful

Therefore I will give him a portion among the great,
> and he will divide the spoils with the strong,
because he poured out his life unto death,
> and was numbered with the transgressors. (Isaiah 53:12)

A dear pastor friend reminded me that Jesus kept his scars for all to see, and I love Him in His woundedness. He gives His love and compassion to me a hundred–fold. I'm on my knees in front of my Lord today and every day. I offer Him all I am and all I have. I hold my hands lifted up to Him. My body may be like a fragile jar of clay, but it carries within it the treasure of love for a hurting world.

God is leading me to authentic people who will not stomp on my heart or use it for their selfish gain. I predict by your grace, my Lord, you are going to move and change my life drastically this year. You have been preparing me for this journey I'm about to embark on.

I was born for this new adventure—to shine more of your love, more of your glory, more of YOU into this broken world. I lay every encounter, every relationship, and every open and closed door at your feet. O the places I'll go! The people I'll meet!

Come to the Party!

Because the Sovereign Lord helps me,
 I will not be disgraced.
Therefore have I set my face like flint,
 and I know I will not be put to shame. (Isaiah 50:7)

God's promises are greater than my problems. I know this. His wisdom refreshes and restores me. Because the sovereign Lord protects me, I will not be ashamed, therefore I will set my face like a stone determined to do his will.

I only desire more of my Father, and those who share this love —more union, more intimacy, everything I can take in to glorify you. You are creating within me an inner party of love and delight to share with the world. My Lord, this year you have become my incredible Father, my closest friend, my greatest love, and my river of life. I am loved! I declare victory before I can see it. I believe I will receive my miracle because my Father is by my side. He gives me a fire in my soul to share with the world. Come to the party!

Prepared for Battle

You armed me with strength for battle; you humbled my adversaries before me. (Psalm 18:39)

Let's look at ourselves. Let's dream big. Let's look at our lives. Let's look at our creative unique selves, for such a time as this. Let's consider the beauty of who we are, called to go beyond our imaginations. Children of God, not directed by manmade rules, but by God's unique calling.

I'm not afraid of this battle anymore. God created me for this. He'll give me everything I need to fight and not grow weary. God is with me. I praise him in the storm.

Determined to Listen

His peace will guard your hearts and minds as you live in Christ Jesus (Philippians 4:7b)

To hear His still, small voice requires special effort; it requires silence, solitude, and a determination to listen. If we do listen to that small voice, we can experience beauty, peace, restoration, and remarkable, extravagant love.

The great news is God's peace shines upon us; these rays of peace transcend understanding. We are to be in close communion with our Father God and then we can give to people who are desperate for his love. And He will guard your hearts and minds as you live in Christ Jesus (Phil. 4:7b).

Dwelling in Weakness

Although he was crucified in weakness, he now lives by the power of God. We, too, are weak, just as Christ was, but when we deal with you we will be alive with him and will have God's power. (2 Corinthians 13:4)

I love talking about "love," but I need to be honest, I am right in the middle of figuring this beautiful love dance out myself. And yes, the dance can be beautiful! We are all in this journey together, listening with prayer, keeping the rhythm of the love of God.

At times we may be forced to our knees in our vulnerability. To love life means to love our vulnerability as we reach out and ask for care, support, guidance, and love. We must remember to capture these moments of our weakness and allow ourselves to dwell in peace and love as we hear our Father say, "You are my Beloved, on you my Favor rests."

Finding Courage in Love

There is no fear in love. But perfect love drives out fear, because fear has to do with punishment. We love because He first loved us. (1 John 4:18a, 19)

In this upside down world, it's easy to adapt to the world's view of love. These worldly messages of what love is (or is not) are conveyed to us on social media, television, magazines, etc. The messages often include the themes of "hold me, touch me, pay attention to me, speak to me, give to me!"

These messages may have an ounce of truth in them, but we spend way too much energy, time, and resources micromanaging our world to adapt to these imposter messages. We exhaust our lives wanting, grasping, and demanding others to fill our love needs when God alone is the only one that can fulfill us.

We must start by realizing that our restless heart's yearning for perfect love can only be met through communion with the One who created us. His perfect love drives out fear and gives us courage to love others fearlessly.

The Powerful Wounded

Be imitators of God, therefore, as dearly loved children and live a life of love, just as Christ loved us and gave himself up for us as a fragrant offering and sacrifice to God. (Ephesians 5:1–2)

Where do we go if our lives have been struck by a wrecking ball? If we have been hit by a friend or loved one who has betrayed us? Who has stolen from us? Abused us and left us under the bus to bleed?

We can find refuge, and I know I do, in knowing that many walk through this life as "wounded healers." They too have been hit by the arrows and assaults of others, but they have become whole in Christ and now live a life of restored beauty, love, and joy. Now, they reach out and love others with a more extravagant love and strength of God they didn't know they had before the trauma and assaults.

They are exceedingly thankful for the battle scars as it pushes them forward in love and consolation, letting them be with the ones who need them. As we're told in Ephesians 5:1–2, we are to be "imitators of God, therefore, as dearly loved children and live a life of love, just as Christ loved us and gave himself up for us as a fragrant offering and sacrifice to God."

Love Revolutionaries

"I am going to take off your chains and let you go . . . I will see that you are well cared for . . . the whole land is before you" (Jeremiah 40:4, NLT)

I have learned to take consolation in the lives of the Saints and today find hope in the healing of Jeremiah's sufferings. When we get self–important, God often gets quiet. The prophet wasn't troubled by the prevalence of people's words, but was deeply sorrowful of the absence of the words of God. When we are screaming with pain, often the intensity of our devotion to our great God and comforter is lost.

In the Scriptures, Jeremiah learned to turn to the God who made him rich with wounds but who was also the only Source of healing. Jeremiah 40: 4 says, "I am going to take off your chains and let you go . . . I will see that you are well cared for . . . the whole land is before you."

God is always beckoning us into a deeper, richer experience of love with him. We can come out of the fire of a broken relationship overwhelmed with joy and love. We can become addicted to all things glorious and then have the great opportunity to give that extravagant, glorious love away as God creates a love revolution through us!

Victory Banner

But thanks be to God, who always leads us as captives in Christ's triumphal procession and uses us to spread the aroma of the knowledge of him everywhere. (2 Corinthians 2:14)

With God's tender heart of love, He has brought me tremendous hope, fresh courage, and a joy that propels me into a great God story. I have learned by faith to relax and let God be God. And as I have learned to do this, I have discovered that Christ holds my life altogether. His cords of hopes, joys, and dreams are woven into a beautiful tapestry by My Abba Father. I worship and rejoice with tears of joy!

He has redeemed me! He has saved me! This tapestry is a Victory Banner. My life is His Victory Banner in this hurting world. You are His Victory Banner. Made whole, marching, and announcing His fame to all who come near.

By His Grace

But we have this treasure in jars of clay to show that this all-surpassing power is from God and not from us. (2 Corinthians 4:7)

I'm on my knees in front of my Lord today. I offer You all I am and all I have. I hold my heart in my hands, lifted up to You. My body may be like a fragile clay jar, but it carries within it the treasure of love for a hurting world. I know you are leading me to authentic people who will not crush my heart or use it for their selfish gain.

I predict, by your grace my Lord, you are going to move and change my life drastically this year. You have been preparing me for this. I was born for this new adventure—to shine more of your love, more of your glory, and more of YOU into this broken world. I lay every encounter, every relationship, every open and closed door at your feet. O the places I'll go! The people I'll meet!

From Devastation to Joy

Because the Sovereign Lord helps me,
 I will not be disgraced.
Therefore have I set my face like flint,
 and I know I will not be put to shame. (Isaiah 50:7)

Only my King could flip the worst year imaginable. On every front—physically, emotionally, financially—and a relationship that tried to destroy me. He flipped it around and completed every promise He spoke to my heart.

I learned to not focus on my problems but God's promises. From devastation to joy! The Lord God has given me his words of wisdom. From incredible fear to tremendous faith. Because the sovereign Lord held me, I will not be disgraced, therefore I will set my face like a stone determined to do his will.

From Disaster to Desire

The Lord will surely comfort Zion and will look with compassion on all her ruins; he will make her deserts like Eden, her wastelands like the garden of the Lord. Joy and gladness will be found in her, thanksgiving and the sound of singing. (Isaiah 51:3)

From disaster to desire. I only desire more of my Father, and those who share this love—more union, more intimacy, everything I can take in to glorify you. You are creating within me an inner party of love and delight to share with the world.

My Lord, you have become my incredible Father, my closest friend, my greatest love, and my river of life. I AM LOVED! I declare victory before I can see it. I believe I will receive my miracle because my Father is by my side. He gives me a fire in my soul to share with the world.

Provision in Disruption

My child, don't reject the Lord's discipline,
    and don't be upset when he corrects you.
For the Lord corrects those he loves,
    just as a father corrects a child in whom he delights
    (Proverbs 3:11–12, NLT)

My greatest worship is in my tears of affliction. God, I know you will give me insight into the disruptive moments. You will help me understand the pain, the provision, the product, and the training of the disruptive moment.

Help me remember, oh Lord, that interruptions are divine instructions. The sting of disruption will disappear as I let go and learn to see you, Lord, in all things.

"I bear witness that I owe more to the fire, and the hammer, and the file, than to anything else in my Lord's workshop. I sometimes question whether I have learned anything except through the rod. When the schoolroom is darkened I see most" – Charles Spurgeon from *Spurgeon's Sermon Notes*, page 307.

Fight and Don't Grow Weary

In your strength I can crush an army; with my God I can scale any wall. (2 Samuel 22:30)

Let's look at ourselves. Let's dream big. Big enough so they will take all the love we can give. Let's look at our lives—our creative unique selves for such a time as this. Not just directed by manmade rules, but God's unique calling.

Let's never use the Bible as an excuse for meanness, but as a means for God to reveal our divine purpose. I'm not afraid of this battle anymore. God created me for this. He'll give me everything I need to fight and not grow weary. God is with me.

Where I Meet the Lord

Are you the one to build me a house to dwell in? (2 Samuel 7:5)

My inner castle is a beautiful vast place where my Savior is expecting me with joy to enter in. It is a beautiful place where I'm able to take time to explore the vast dimensions of God's love. I've visited this place before. There have been many small trips, but also two extended ones—first when I had cancer and then a traumatic brain injury—filled with rich treasures that awaited me. He calls me to create, desire, and dream in this castle.

When I go to the innermost recesses of my soul, Joy awaits! I let go of the pleasure in external objects and enter into the presence of my dearest friend. It's just He and I, loving one another and dreaming. He shows me more desires and a renewed deeper calling; we vision hope and dream together.

What others might see as a time of despair, I view as a time of deepening joy in the arms of my Father. Enter into times of testing as a place to know God in richer, fuller, wonderful ways. He will meet you there.

Filling Up the Canyon

You make known to me the path of life; you will fill me with joy in your presence. (Psalm 16:11 and Acts 2:28)

The chasm of love within me is so vast, but My Lord fills me up even more extravagantly and lavishly. As I pour myself into prayer for others, God pours more of Himself into my little self. Love attracts love. I shall dare to ask that you my friends will experience more love than I or you could ever comprehend or imagine.

God increases my courage to love in greater proportion to my sufferings. As I fear, God's strength increases within me. I have no capacity for kindness and grace on my own, but My Lord fills me with His compassion. I long and thirst to go to that place where I empty myself and wait for His Love. Mystery and wonder waits there.

One small soul has incredible power. As my Lord becomes one with my heart, we then can pardon a thousand criminals.

Greater Possibilities of Love

But I am like an olive tree flourishing in the house of God; I trust in God's unfailing love for ever and ever. (Psalm 52:8)

Let yourself be drawn into greater possibilities of more love. The wonder of hidden dreams and desires await. Redemption, transformation, and restoration will become fully known as the Father, King, and Romancer pours more of the Kingdom of God within you, giving you an eternal prescription for a life well lived with the divine intimate presence.

This intimate presence is so rich and profound within me, I sometimes blush as my God expresses his tender romantic love to me. He instructs me with renewed passion and direction for the rest of this adventure of life. I am speechless in the beauty and wonder I see.

We have been given the gift of the suffering Christ that awaits and welcomes us Home. His divine Spirit gives language to the risen Christ of Hope and Joy awaiting within us. As He builds his house in our hearts, He draws and beckons us to more love. Let us burst forth with profound gratefulness.

Beyond Making Life Work

I pray that you, being rooted and established in love, may have power, together with all the Lord's holy people, to grasp how wide and long and high and deep is the love of Christ. (Eph. 3:17b–18)

When we make the conscious decision to abandon all, instead of being satisfied with "just making life work," then joy, peace, and love begin to rain down on us like a waterfall. We become soaked in love. We give the drudgery of life over to God and pure joy is set free. We may appear odd to others as we are wildly in love with our Savior. We become overwhelmed with joy when we realize there is no fear in God's love!

As Mary "kept all these things in her heart" (Luke 2:51), we too take a leap of faith and take all questions and fears to God. We ponder in a deep, profound way the voice of God in the depths of our being. We begin to believe in love when it isn't deserved, see hope when everything feels hopeless, and believe in peace in the middle of chaos.

Go and Be Blessed

Whether you turn to the right or to the left, your ears will hear a voice behind you, saying, "This is the way; walk in it." (Isaiah 30:21)

We receive our blessings where God calls us to go. As it says in Isaiah 6:3, "He equips us in this place." Our best weapon is to hear with our hearts the voice of God. He will protect, lead, and restore all that has been taken. Jeremiah 29:11 says, "I know the plans for you, says the Lord God, plans for a future and a hope!"

As I look at the Scriptures, I see that God has a plan made just for me. I don't want to miss out on God's best for me. "This is the way walk ye in it!" (Isaiah 30:21). When we walk with the Spirit in our calling, and when the enemy comes, the Lord will raise up a barrier against Him. When God gives us a vision, He will make the path clear for us.

Third Heaven

I know a man in Christ who fourteen years ago was caught up to the third heaven. Whether it was in the body or out of the body I do not know—God knows. And I know that this man—whether in the body or apart from the body I do not know, but God knows—was caught up to paradise and heard inexpressible things, things that no one is permitted to tell. (2 Corinthians 12:2–4)

This third heaven is where I long to reside. It is the place of protection, this dwelling place where I experience true intimacy and love like I could never comprehend, a place of glorious fellowship.

Stay here in the third heaven! This dwelling place with God! As we are united with our Lord, He reminds us of the many graces that He gives us. I have to admit I am in awe and wonder of this third heaven.

When the storms come crashing in, He calls me back to this place. I'm not afraid to love in this place. I am brave to go the extra mile because in this place I experience an extra measure of grace and love. Nothing can drag me down or discourage me in this place.

Joy Remains

But let all who take refuge in you be glad; let them ever sing for joy. Spread your protection over them, that those who love your name may rejoice in you. (Psalm 5:11)

In 2005, I fell off a bike and suffered a traumatic brain injury that included two subdural hematomas. People have died from this injury and those that live often struggle with horrible headaches, severe depression, and other problems. By the grace of God and love of many, I never had the headaches that many endure, but I only felt and continue to feel incredible joy.

Early in 2016, I had another brain surgery to remove an aggressively growing tumor. Once again, I chose joy over fear. This tumor was totally unrelated to my previous injuries. The only common denominator is that God instilled pure, sweet joy and love in me once again.

A month after surgery, I had a big ugly scar across my forehead that I hid with hats. During that difficult time, God brought a number of prayer warriors my way to pray for me. After a short time, I took off the bandage and low and behold, the scar was not to be seen anywhere! I literally have no scar to this day. More joy! Even if the scar remained, joy would have remained even more. With Christ, there is joy beyond what this world can see or understand.

Worship in My Tears

Guide me in your truth and teach me, for you are God my Savior, and my hope is in you all day long. (Psalm 25:5)

I have come to know in an intimate, beautiful way that the kingdom of God is in the depths of who I am. When life suddenly turns upside down, I find the deepest place of worship is in my tears. And in these tears, God comforts, He guides, and He gives me strength. He is more intimate and nearer than anything and anyone I have ever known.

In this adversity I have found a vast richness of incredible love as I sweetly surrender to Him. Instead of wondering why, I have learned to ask, "What?" O Lord, what do you want me to do? What Lord, do you want to teach me?

Free Indeed

Weeping may stay for the night, but rejoicing comes in the morning. (Psalm 30:5)

I weep. I weep in pain; I weep with loss; I weep with grace; I weep with love; I weep with joy. I weep because I can. I weep because of grace and because it's downright incredible to be alive.

And I'll be free indeed. I am devoted to my personal, everlasting relationship with Jesus Christ. I do not want to live for anything else. As it says in Acts 26:16, "I have appeared unto thee for this purpose" (KJV).

I'm a colorful wildflower that is filled with excitement to bloom and I know who holds my future. As my weeping turns into joyful delight, I happily anticipate following His will, spiritual wisdom and understanding because He promises to give when we ask. Hope for tomorrow comes with incredible joy in the morning. Joy to see more of my love, my Savior.

Defined by the Mess No More

Do not be afraid; you will not be put to shame. Do not fear disgrace; you will not be humiliated. You will forget the shame of your youth ... (Isaiah 54:4)

During a flight home from visiting family, I didn't feel very well. As the plane went up, so did my stomach! As soon as I got into the Atlanta airport, I ran and barely made it to the bathroom where I vomited all over the floor and sinks. I didn't make it to the stall.

I crawled to my next flight. I made it to my window seat where there was a woman dressed in a beautiful pink suit and pink shoes. I just looked at her as my heart sunk. I said to her, "Ma'am, you look so pretty, but I can't sit next to you because I'm a mess."

My flu lasted another week once I arrived home. As I was recovering, and feeling sorry for myself, I began to think of how messy my life has been. Mess defines my life. But it doesn't define me, not anymore. The Lord defines me.

Unlikely and Amazing

Don't judge by his appearance or height, for I have rejected him. The Lord doesn't see things the way you see them. People judge by outward appearance, but the Lord looks at the heart.
(1 Samuel 16:7, NLT)

I am the most unlikely person in the world. By unlikely, I mean, by definition: "not likely to happen, be done, or be true; improbable, questionable, doubtful, debatable, unwanted."

I was abused. When I was a little girl and through my teenage years, I was very angry. The neighbors called me the little red-haired brat. I was the chief of sinners, a runaway, and I aborted two babies.

On many occasions, I tried to commit suicide. Three of my uncles pulled the trigger. That's what my family did when things were tough—we checked out by killing ourselves. Thankfully, I never had the courage to walk completely off the ledge.

I began to see that maybe, just maybe, God could redeem "The Most Unlikely to be Likely."

God uses unlikely people in unlikely places to do unlikely things. I've seen and done and experienced many things in my life, many tragedies, many joys, and many sorrows. He uses the unlikely to do the unbelievable and the unimaginable.

Victory from Faith

But God chose the foolish things of the world to shame the wise; God chose the weak things of the world to shame the strong. (1 Cor. 1:27)

When I was 28, I asked God, "What is my vocation?" He quickly and simply said, "Your vocation is to love, simply love." This was the most special gift he could ever give me. He had given me the gift of love, pure love. My calling since then has been to bring the Divine glory of God around the world.

I am an unlikely woman with an unlikely calling with an unlikely outcome. Like David, who had great faith in an extraordinary God, I trust in Him to love me and use me in astounding ways. Yes, I have had cancer and traumatic brain injury. My faith brings victory even when it seems unlikely. God has given me and formed in me impossible dreams that He keeps making real.

Do you feel broken, messed up, an unlikely candidate with a huge heart of faith? Are you filled with a whole lot of God? Are you "unlikely?" Then you are a great candidate to cling tightly to God while He accomplishes impossible dreams for you and through you.

Face the Anxiety

Be still before the Lord
>and wait patiently for him;
do not fret when people succeed in their ways,
>when they carry out their wicked schemes. (Psalm 37:7)

Anxieties can become overwhelming and may drive us to respond to life out of our pain. The pain can become very destructive. I have become aware of my own anxieties, the anxieties of that little girl that churns with pain and loneliness.

But God has been gracious to me. He has taught me that instead of stuffing that anxiety and pain, I should acknowledge it, feel it, and ask Christ into the depths of the pain and loneliness.

And the most amazing miraculous process has been happening in me as I do this. The loneliness is leaving. Even when I am alone, I don't seem to feel alone. I feel God. A whole lot of God. But, in order to feel this, I had to be still and listen to God. It is so easy to run away from our pain and loneliness. Face it, and ask God to overcome it through you. Be still and let Him fight the war within.

Depravity Defeated

But the tax collector stood at a distance. He would not even look up to heaven, but beat his breast and said, "God, have mercy on me, a sinner." (Luke 18:13)

We often make unhealthy choices to drive away our anxieties, to pretend they don't exist. But really, when we make these impulsive, unhealthily choices, it multiplies our anxieties and soon we feel out of control.

In this out-of-control state we get pushed into despair. The despair breeds depression and as the depression grows, we find ourselves smack in the middle of our own depravity. If we can acknowledge that place of utter depravity in ourselves, it can catapult us to our greatest place of worship, the place where we cease pretending we're something that we're not, let go of our pride and self-sufficiency, and invite God in. This is when worship happens.

Living in the Seam

My soul thirsts for God, for the living God. When can I go and meet with God? (Psalm 42:2)

To arrive at worship and relief from our anxieties, we must go away to a deserted place. Away from the hustle and bustle of life. We need to wait, watch, and truly listen. If we are patient, we can enter the thin place between heaven and earth.

What is a "thin place"? Richard Rohr, a Franciscan priest, author, speaker and spiritual leader relates living on the spiritual edge as living in a "thin place." For me, it is a deep, profound, and intimate place where the distance between heaven and earth evaporates and I'm able to catch glimpses of the Divine. It is a seam between this world and eternity.

Traveling to it can often feel disorientating. We can feel confused. We can lose our bearings, and find a new normal. We are jolted out of old ways of seeing the world, and therein lay the transformative magic of the sacred.

Breathtaking on the Edge

For I am the Lord your God who takes hold of your right hand and says to you, Do not fear; I will help you. (Isaiah 41:13)

I have experienced these beautiful, captivating thin places, like walking a tightrope between loss and surrender. It is breathtaking and far beyond anything you can ever imagine. Sometimes these moments appear through an ordinary reality.

My son Wesley was hurt badly in a soccer game. He tore his ACL and meniscus. This happened right before his senior year as the team captain. I was so worried about him—this horrible event turned his life upside down in every way. I went to bed weeping, and begging, "Please God, please help him! He needs a miracle."

God woke me about 4 a.m. and said in a comforting. pleading way, "Julie, you can trust me with Wesley. I am guiding him into a new direction. Trust me with your son." I was so consumed with worry, but God gave me the comfort I needed to trust Him that my son was going to be alright.

That was a thin place, on the edge of what I could endure, but perfectly positioned to receive God's grace and strength. At the end of myself, but at the beginning of Him. Don't fear going to that place. He will meet you. Wait and trust.

Julie Woodley is director of Restoring the Heart Ministries (www. rthm.cc), serving childhood sexual abuse victims and post-abortion women. Her story has aired on *The 700 Club*, *Focus on the Family*, *Life Today*, and *Dr. James Dobson's familytalk*. She is the author of *A Wildflower Grows in Brooklyn* (2013), co-author of *Surviving the Storms of Life* (2008), and the producer of *In the Wildflowers* and *Into My Arms* counseling DVDs. She is an ordained and licensed minister in the International Ministerial Fellowship, licensed Christian counselor, and certified trauma counselor. She serves as a group facilitator at the Leyden DuPage Clinic (Naperville, IL). She was inducted into the Suffolk County (NY) Women's Hall of Fame (2009) and has received numerous other awards. Julie has four children and five grandchildren.

www.ingramcontent.com/pod-product-compliance
Lightning Source LLC
Chambersburg PA
CBHW061303040426
42444CB00010B/2497